Saff Gets a Dress

By Carmel Reilly

It's Saff!

Saff will get a dress
with Dad.

Saff puts on this dress, but it's too big.

It will not fit!

"This red dress will fit, Saff,"
said Dad.

"No! Red is not fab,"
said Saff.

"Do not get in a huff, Saff,"
said Dad.
"This dress is not red!"

"We can cut the cuffs off!"
said Dad.

"The cuffs are fab!"
said Saff.
"But the dress is stiff!"

cuffs

"This dress is not stiff, Saff," said Dad.

"Will it fit, Saff?" said Dad.

"It will look fab," said Dad.
"But you did huff a **lot**!"

CHECKING FOR MEANING

1. What did Saff say about the red dress? *(Literal)*

2. What did Dad suggest doing to the dress with the cuffs? *(Literal)*

3. What did Dad mean when he said, *But you did huff a **lot**!? (Inferential)*

EXTENDING VOCABULARY

dress	Look at the word *dress*. If you took away the letters *d* and *r*, what other letter or letters could you put at the start to make a new word? E.g. less, mess.
cuffs	What are *cuffs*? What is the purpose of cuffs? How else do we use this word, other than for clothing?
stiff	What does it mean if a dress is *stiff*? How would a stiff dress feel to wear? If a dress was the opposite of stiff, what words could you use to describe it? E.g. soft, floating, smooth.

MOVING BEYOND THE TEXT

1. Who chooses the clothes you wear? Why?

2. If you were buying a new outfit, what would you want it to look like?

3. When you wear your favourite outfit, how does it make you feel?

4. How can we recycle clothes so they don't end up in landfill?

SPEED SOUNDS

ff	ll	ss	zz

PRACTICE WORDS

will

Saff

dress

cuffs

huff

off

Will

stiff